About the Author

Neil Cameron has directed theatre and arts events with the community for over twenty years and in that time has produced eighty-four major productions. He has worked mainly in England, Scotland and Australia but also in Japan, Holland, Germany, Canada, USA and New Zealand. Two of his productions have won the 'Event of the Year' in the Northern Territory and he was also the director of the Melbourne Peace Vigil Festival which won a United Nations Peace Award for Australia.

He came to Melbourne as a Gulbenkian Scholarship recipient in 1981 and has lived in Australia since then. He is well known for his large-scale ceremonies which include community involvement and large and spectacular visual effects using fire, music and fireworks. These events have been presented to over 60,000 people in the last two years. In 1993 his book *Fire on the Water,* a personal view of theatre and community, was published by Currency Press.

Neil Cameron travels widely, lecturing on theatre in the community and lives in Maleny, Queensland.

D1518579

THE
RUNNING
AND
STAMPING
BOOK

NEIL CAMERON

Illustrated by
FARIDAH WHYTE

HEINEMANN
PORTSMOUTH, NEW HAMPSHIRE

FOR THE CHILDREN
OF MY FAMILY
◆

HARLEY, ARIFAH, LATIF,
SARAH, MUZZ, LUKE AND POLLY,
WHO HAVE KEPT ME RUNNING ABOUT
FOR YEARS.

Contents

◆

Introduction

◆

NOW, HERE, YOU SEE, IT TAKES ALL THE
RUNNING YOU CAN DO, TO KEEP IN THE SAME
PLACE. IF YOU WANT TO GET SOMEWHERE ELSE,
YOU MUST RUN AT LEAST TWICE AS FAST AS
THAT!

LEWIS CARROLL

For some years now I have been using running and stamping
for warm-ups when teaching theatre to students. It started as
a single running exercise shown to me by Melbourne-based
theatre teacher John Bolton some ten years ago. Gradually I
developed more exercises until a series of forty emerged
which I would use when working with performers. Many
students asked for copies of the exercises and I decided to
write them down, hoping they might be useful to other
teachers. They can be used in conjunction with other types of
exercises or as a series on their own.

I wanted to find a type of exercise that 'woke up' the student
before the work of creating theatre started. I do not mean that
I just wanted to shake off a night's sleep but to truly 'awaken'
them to the creative experience. I wanted to find a process
that separated them from the kind of consciousness that living
day to day in a city produces. I wanted them to be open, joyful,
bright-eyed, concentrated on the group, dancing.

As the running and stamping exercises developed I found
that they were a wonderful way of getting students fit. Over a
month the students improve in stamina, physical strength and
muscular coordination. The exercises also generate a strong
feeling amongst the group and the regular sessions bring
about a sense of solidarity and common aim.

Some of the exercises are designed to create calm and
harmony within the group, others to build trust, cooperation
and group unity. Another set of exercises was constructed to

develop theatre skills in movement, voice and the use of the body. A last group develops a feeling of energy, excitement and joy.

I include the stamping exercises for those who are particularly interested in physical theatre techniques. All can be used to develop dramatic or dance forms, script, physical movement and even performance.

The stamping exercises developed as a response to watching Aboriginal dancers in the Northern Territory who use stamping as a basis to many of their dances. I often work in physically based theatre and I found that stamping transfers the actor's sense of energy and balance from their minds into their bodies and puts them back in touch with the earth.

Suzuki, the Japanese theatre director has used stamping exercises as a method of training:

> *In stamping, we come to understand that the body establishes its relationship to the ground through the feet, that the ground and the body are not two separate entities. We are part of the ground. Our very beings will return to the earth when we die.*

These exercises work better over a longer period and as each day goes past they grow in strength and power. I have put in forty exercises but of course the variations are endless. I hope this book will inspire others to invent their own exercises.

DISCLAIMER

These exercises are developed for warming up performers. They should at no time be used with any strain on the individuals concerned or used in a competitive way. They are designed for groups who have attained a certain standard of fitness before they start and the author takes no responsibility for any injury or harm sustained during these exercises.

It must always be remembered that running is a natural healthy pastime but can be dangerous to anyone who has an injury, a medical condition or is unfit.

PART ONE

Preparations

STILL AS THEY RUN AND LOOK BEHIND,
THEY HEAR A VOICE IN EVERY WIND
AND SNATCH A FEARFUL JOY.

THOMAS GRAY

In 1969 I was invited to stay in a Zen monastery near Mount Aso on the island of Kyushu in southern Japan. It was a beautiful monastery many hundreds of years old. It had a great number of buildings including a large temple set in the middle of perfect Japanese gardens. The whole complex had at one time been home to four hundred monks, but now there were only forty. I was awoken every morning at three and taken sleepily through pitch black gardens and brought to the door of the great temple. I was told to sit down and watch the proceedings within.

There were hundreds of candles and lanterns lighting up the vast hall of the temple. The floor area was clear except for a small altar in the middle. Huge clouds of incense were being swung through the air as the monks gathered and silently stood in a circle around the altar. Suddenly a gong that must have been at least twelve feet across sounded and the monks began to run round the hall. They were chanting old Chinese hymns and their voices echoed through the cavernous space. The monks' feet could be heard tapping out the rhythm of the songs. This went on for an hour as the sun slowly rose. When the monks eventually finished their ceremony, they left the temple laughing and talking, invigorated, to meet the day.

The memory of these men led me to develop these exercises.

In our ancestral past running was essential to our survival and our ability to run far and fast was a prerequisite to living. Hunters had to outrun their prey and in times of danger all messages had to be sent by runner. The very existence of the community depended on the power of the runner.

In ancient Greece runners were trained from a group of men called *hemerodromi*, the most famous of whom was Philippides. He took a message from Athens to Sparta asking for help against a force of invading Persians. He ran the 150 miles in a couple of days. Another messenger was sent back to Athens with a message of victory after the battle of Marathon – a distance of 24 miles. This incident, of course, lead to the birth of the modern marathon.

The Persian couriers of the Turkish sultans often ran from Constantinople to Adrianople and back, a distance of about 220 miles in two days and nights.

Zulu troops could run up to thirty miles a day carrying arms. There are reports of being able to hear their singing and their feet beating the ground from many miles away.

But for the modern man or woman running is not necessarily part of life and it is therefore necessary to prepare carefully before engaging in the following exercises.

I have laid out below a number of points which should be read carefully before starting classes. If you would like further information there are many books on running which include details of safety measures. Your local department responsible for sport should be able to supply you with pamphlets on safety procedures and people who can give advice.

THE PLACE

I would like to describe the place where I most enjoy teaching running and stamping. It is a large hall about the size of a basketball court. It has sprung wooden floors in good condition and has been cleaned until it shines. The windows are tall and let in streaming light and the doors, if they are left open, let in the sound of birdsong.

Finding such a space is not always possible and a less beautiful space would be quite sufficient. However I believe that these exercises open up the students to their inner selves and the atmosphere of the hall will be important in this process. Light, space, the texture of the floor, the number of students will all be important factors.

THE NUMBER OF STUDENTS

In a space the size of a basketball court the ideal number is about twenty but one can work with less. With more, the size of the space would have to increase but I would only work with larger numbers if the students had worked on these exercises earlier in smaller groups. Large numbers of beginners would be difficult to handle.

For some of the exercises an even number of students is necessary and if the numbers need rounding I run as a student.

THE ROLE OF THE TEACHER

Once the class starts, the running or stamping continues throughout and students do not stop. A gentle rhythm is maintained right through the class.

I plan each class carefully and come in prepared but I am very open to change. I go with the energy of the situation. If I see something new and valuable developing I let it gain momentum and if this means abandoning my previous plan so be it. The exercises in this book have developed with the help of the students – so often they have taken the initiative and sprung into something new or suggested a variation which has led to a better way of doing it.

The choice of exercise is something best left to each teacher to decide. I have put the simpler, get-fit exercises first and these can be repeated many times before moving on to others. Some exercises might be shortened and used in concert with others or certain ones might become staples, being used regularly in between others. The choice lies with the teacher.

It is the teacher's role to tune in deeply to the rhythm of the group and to watch carefully for the state of each individual within it. As with all classes, the state of mind of the group changes with each day. Mondays for example are harder after a weekend break and many other local conditions can affect the group. I respond to each situation as quickly as possible and again, will abandon my original plan for a better one if necessary. The group might need an exercise that improves group solidarity or need to let off steam or conversely there might be a need for an exercise that calms and centres.

After working with the group for some time it can be quite clear when a particular individual is not participating with the rest. I watch carefully for this and, slowly running beside them, have a quiet word. Non-participation can be totally unrelated to the group – a personal situation or a physical problem – or it can be about their relationships or work situation with the other students. Whatever the cause happens to be, the teacher should try to sort such problems out as even one individual's energy can affect a group's psychology in an adverse way.

Once the class has started any students arriving late are asked to stay outside until the class is over. The classes should start as a group and late-comers disturb the rhythm.

As a teacher I run throughout the class. I keep to my own rhythm which sometimes synthesises with the group and at other times goes on its own journey. I feel this is very important for my teaching; whether this will be shared with other teachers I will leave for them to decide.

> TO WATCH A... RUNNER... CAN BE A BEAUTIFUL EXPERIENCE. THE RUNNER'S MOVEMENTS FLOW... EYES ARE SET AND STARRY... FEET SEEM TO MERGE DYNAMICALLY WITH THE GROUND AND THE AIR... BODY APPEARS TO ALMOST FLOAT.
>
> **GERRY EGGER**

SOUND

It must be agreed that there is to be no talking between students throughout the exercises unless the teacher asks. The central rhythm is very important to the feeling of the group as is the feeling of silence and calm. This cannot be achieved if people are talking.

However, the use of music or percussion of different types, either external to the group or played by the group can be very important. All the exercises in the book can be accompanied by the appropriate music but I believe that it is important to do the exercises in a quiet atmosphere to begin with.

PREPARATION FOR THE CLASSES

If the students are given notice prior to the sessions then they can take up a little jogging each morning. There are many good books which lay out the basic safety matters.

No one should attempt any sort of running without seeing a doctor if they have any doubts about their fitness on any level.

No special diet is needed to do any of the exercises in this book but heavy meals are not recommended before starting.

FEET

The students must run with bare feet. This is vital to the process. It is important for the participants to 'feel' the surface under the soles of their feet. In cold weather they may be reluctant to do this, but the exercises will soon warm the feet up.

CLOTHES

The students can wear any form of loose clothing – as they would in normal warm-ups. Old t-shirts, track suits and the like are perfect but their suitability will vary from climate to climate. It is important that after the exercises are over students do not get cold – they should have sweaters and socks at the ready if the weather is inclement. No shoes or socks are worn for any of the exercises.

FLOOR

The floor is important. As the students build up fitness and stamina they can find themselves running quite a distance each day. This is not good to do if the surface is bad. Concrete for example could be damaging in the long term to bare feet. A great deal of care must be taken to see that the runners do not injure themselves during the exercises.

The floor must always be clean and free from anything that might injure the feet. It should be washed at the beginning of each week by the students and swept each morning before work by the students. I believe it is important for them to do this job as it guarantees a job well done and further increases awareness of the floor's surface – the surface which they are using in such a specialised way.

TIME

When I start the students off for the first week I keep the exercise time down to twenty minutes, slowly increasing to about forty-five minutes. Each group is different and I gauge the time on their ability. It is vital to stop before they get tired and to build up a little each day until an exercise time is reached which suits the whole class.

General fitness aside, some exercises can be extended if they are developing and others cut short as they lose energy. The main guideline is not to over extend the session nor to finish too quickly. Each teacher will be able to judge the situation with each class.

SAFETY

Physical safety should always be of paramount importance.

The first aspect of this relates to the general fitness of the group. One is going to be asking these people to run a large distance over the time allotted; their ability to do this must be carefully assessed. The group must NEVER be put through any strain. These are warm-up exercises and it completely defeats the purpose to have exhausted or injured students before the main work of the day has begun. Each day must be taken gently and the load increased without physical stress or injury. This is the most important factor in these exercises and it is much better to experience too little than too much.

When I get a group together I ask them to tell me about ANY physical injuries or complaints before we start. Obviously foot or leg injuries can be exacerbated by running and stamping, as can back problems. The teacher must decide whether each student has passed the 'fitness test' before they are allowed to take part in the class.

I also 'look' at the participants one by one. I really try to get a feel as to their general fitness. Although they might not have any specific injury, their general condition due to age or way of life might make their involvement dangerous to their physical welfare. I always keep a close eye on any who might be under more strain than the others and stop them before damage occurs. This problem diminishes as the group gets fitter.

WITH PRACTICE RUNNING BECOMES INCREASINGLY EFFORTLESS AT TIMES. MENTAL RESISTANCE, BODY AILMENTS AND WEAKNESS FADE AWAY OR BECOME UTTERLY FAMILIAR. ONE IS LAUNCHED, DETACHED FROM THE ORDINARY.

JIM SHAPIRO

The students' safety and well-being are in the teacher's hands and that trust must be honoured with the greatest attention. Because of these exercises' physical nature it is vital to maintain complete discipline at all times to avoid injury.

If there is a fall or someone strains a muscle or a joint then it is important to withdraw them from the class at once. A first-aid kit should ALWAYS be available and medical assistance called for if necessary.

The teacher is responsible for the class and should determine the best course of action.

THE EGO

The ego can lead to injury. These exercises are not about running fast or far. No one can do better than any one else. There must be NO competition, and any signs of students trying to beat others should be immediately dealt with. It is counter to everything that these classes stand for.

Fred Roche said in *The Zen of Running*:

so one aspect of running meditation
is the sheer joy right now of this running
another aspect
is the learning process
which uses this as a metaphor
for the rest of my life
whatever you do
with your running
you cheat yourself
by pushing, pressing, competing
there are no standards
and no possible victories except
the joy you are living
while dancing your run
in any life
joy is the known
in this moment-now

OTHER PLACES

Once the group is familiar with some, or all of the exercises, it is wonderful to go out of the hall into some new environment. The exercises have to be adapted to the new situation but most can be repeated as they were practised in the hall.

Running along the beach or through grass, through the woods and round the sides of the hills are all a joy once the group has become fit and attuned to the exercises.

A first-aid kit should be carried and plenty to drink. The teacher should be aware that in some cases the physical hardships have greatly increased by going outside and allowance must be made for these. Footwear should be considered if the outside surface is in any way dangerous. Check all running surfaces for broken glass and other dangerous objects.

PART TWO

The Running

THE MOUNTAINS, I BECAME PART OF IT...
THE HERBS, THE FIR TREE, I BECAME PART OF IT.
THE MORNING MISTS, THE CLOUDS, THE GATHERING WATERS,
I BECAME PART OF IT.
THE WILDERNESS, THE DEW DROPS, THE POLLEN...
I BECAME PART OF IT.

NAVAJO CHANT

I have always loved running and find that it is a free-flowing movement which frees the muscles of the body and develops strength, fitness and stamina.

I met Australian theatre director Richard Davy when he was in Edinburgh many years ago where he was teaching Aboriginal running. I stayed with him in Tasmania when I first arrived in Australia in 1981. Waking to a beautiful morning and with the rest of the house sleeping, I pulled on my jogging shoes and trotted gently on to the path leading away into the sunrise. Richard's dog had seen me and was joyfully running at my ankles, pleasantly surprised by his luck. I was running freely, breathing regularly, body moving without strain. It was a glorious morning, the fields glittering with dew, the huge Huon pines towering above me every way I looked, birds flashing with colour as they streaked through the clear air. The world was awake and was celebrating. The ground started to slope upwards and a fair-sized hill came into view. Usually the body starts to feel the strain pulling up a hill, but this morning it seemed effortless.

Energy surged through my body and I increased my speed. The slope meant nothing, my legs sang with strength, my breath came rhythmically without effort and I felt that I could run anywhere – forever. I began to lose a sense of my body and I became integrated into the bush around me. I lost myself and became smooth flowing energy. The top of the hill came into view and I accelerated up to full-speed running. I stopped at the crest, my body singing with the joy of movement. I was jumping and whooping. The land opened out below me in a view that stretched thirty miles in every direction. The mists were clearing – leaving the world clear and fresh.

Introduction to
the Running Exercises

◆

WE SWING UNGIRDED HIPS,
AND LIGHTENED ARE OUR EYES,
THE RAIN IS ON OUR LIPS,
WE DO NOT RUN FOR PRIZE

WE RUN BECAUSE WE LIKE IT
THROUGH THE BROAD BRIGHT LAND.

FROM SONG OF THE UNGIRT RUNNERS
BY CHARLES HAMILTON SORLEY

IT DON'T MEAN A THING IF IT AIN'T GOT THAT SWING.

DUKE ELLINGTON

AIMS

I try to aim towards a non-thinking state, a sort of moving meditation, where the body has taken over, working mechanically, to clear the students' minds of their personal lives and their attendant cares and troubles – the hassles getting to class, the traffic, the strain. When the group starts running the physical activity itself will fully occupy the mind, but as time goes by and the individuals get fitter, then different exercises with added dimensions become possible. I have included a number of what I have called contemplative runs which are useful in concentrating energy. The run itself becomes a meditative experience.

These exercises can be adapted and used in any order and in any combination but I have laid out the exercises in the order that I do them when I start with a new group. I do change the basic order when I feel it needs adapting. However, the order as presented has been evolved through practice, trial and error.

The methods of giving instruction to the group are important. As the students are running in silence (unless the teacher instructs otherwise) it is relatively easy to be heard. Instructions should be carefully explained until everyone understands, then a clear signal – by word of mouth, a drum beat, clapper sticks or a hand clap – given as the signal to change into another pattern. A whistle should be avoided.

The Aztecs gave the following advice to students:

When thou art summoned, be not summoned twice... [go] the very first time... arise quickly... [be] prompt... swift... [and] in no wise sluggish; like the wind art thou to go [and] be diligent [lest thou] be considered as... a haughty one.

NOTE: *Throughout this book I have assumed the number of students in the group to be twenty.*

The Snake

IT'S NORTH YOU MAY RUN TO THE
   RIME-RINGED SUN,
OR SOUTH TO THE BLIND HORN'S HATE;
OR EAST ALL THE WAY INTO MISSISSIPPI BAY,
OR WEST TO THE GOLDEN GATE.

RUDYARD KIPLING

Every exercise class should start and finish with this basic run. The class meets standing in a circle. A volunteer starts running in any direction around the edge of the room and the rest follow in a line. The leader changes each day. The students are asked to run gently around the edge of the hall at a slow, relaxed regular pace, keeping a space between the end of the group and the front runner and running without crowding the person in front.

Every few minutes the teacher asks the leader to move to the back of the group giving someone else a chance to lead.

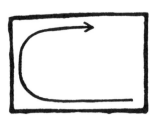

(You will see that each person runs in a different way and this is often reflected in the rest of the group. It is therefore important to change leaders regularly.)

The runners are now running around the hall, arms moving smoothly, breath increased but not strained, feet padding lightly on the floor. There is no sound except the light drumming of feet.

The group might be running in a clockwise direction with the right side of their bodies leaning slightly into the room as they turn the corners. To maintain balance in the body so that they are not always leaning in the same direction it is desirable to change direction. This is done simply by the leader, who changes from clockwise to anti-clockwise, by diagonally crossing the hall and running in the other direction. This should be done every few minutes.

When the session is finished the group slows down gradually to a gentle pace and at the same time closes the gap between the leader and the last student until a circle is formed. They are asked to reduce speed to walking pace and then come to a stop as one. This is done without any sound with the group determining the pace.

Once they have stopped they are back as they started – in a circle.

NOTE: *Remember that this exercise starts and finishes every exercise.*

Moving Around the Room

◆

THE THINKING, THE CONTEMPLATIVE SIDE,
THE INTELLECTUALISING, RUNNERS RESIST
BECAUSE YOU RUN FOR THE RUNNING, NOT
TO REFLECT ABOUT IT LATER.

KENNY MOORE

Start with *the snake* (see Exercise 1) – until every student has had a chance to lead. If they seem to be struggling make sure they slow down and relax. To do this, ask them to totally relax their arms so that they are hanging down, swinging gently. Ask them to note what happens when their arms work again. Relax shoulders, then work normally again, relax other parts of the body and find out where tension is occurring and try to ease off. Keep breathing regularly – 'no strain' are the words to convey.

Watch that the group is not going too fast. Now the leader is asked to go into a random pattern. Now the snake becomes

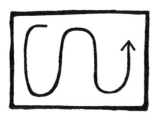

truly mobile, snaking all over the room. The leaders continue to change as each person makes an individual pattern on the floor. These snaking movements can be an experiment with tight turns or long circling movements.

A development of this is a sort of 'follow-my-leader' where the leader changes the way they run in some chosen way and the rest of the group have to follow suit.

Then the snake is asked to come slowly down to running on the spot without banging into anyone. Now close up the gaps between the students until they are almost touching. They put their hands on the shoulders of the student in front – they can give a quick shoulder massage before moving off. When the group feels confident they slowly move forward around the room. After a while arms can come down and they can continue in close formation. Then back to normal.

This can be repeated as many times as is judged appropriate.

Finish with *the snake*, slowing to a halt as in Exercise 1.

Greeting

◆

WE TWA HAE RUN ABOUT THE BRAES,
AND PU'D THE GOWANS FINE

WE'LL TAK' A RIGHT GUDE WILLIE WAUGHT
FOR AULD LANG SYNE.

ROBERT BURNS

The session commences with *the snake*, which the group keeps up for several minutes – then starts moving around in any direction, as each leader decides. When the runners feel comfortable they start running around the hall in the regular way.

The leader reaches the end of the hall and turns sharply so that the line is led back along itself. This continues in a tight snaking movement across the hall and then back to running the normal route around the hall. This tight snaking movement is repeated until the group is confident.

Next, as they come in to the sharp turn at the ends of the classroom the runners put up their hands so that they can lightly touch the hands of the part of the line they are passing.

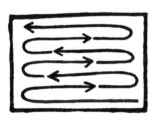

This continues across the hall while there is room. It is repeated and this time they say 'good morning' to each other as they touch hands. Even at a slow speed the greetings have to be quick. The greetings can be said in any language or in any manner.

Then back to *the snake* and a normal finish.

Running as Two

EXCEPT IN THE CASE OF SUPER-RIGOROUS TRAINING, RUNNING MAKES PEOPLE LOOK AND FEEL SEXIER. IT HEIGHTENS SENSUALITY, INCREASES SEXUAL ENERGY AND IMPROVES RACE PERFORMANCE. IN MOST CASES, SEX DOESN'T INTERFERE IN RUNNING, OR RUNNING WITH SEX – UNLESS YOU TRY TO DO BOTH AT ONCE.

MICHAEL CASTLEMAN

The class starts off with five minutes of *the snake* and slows down to running on the spot. Counting down the line the teacher asks the eleventh student to lead a second group and to run up parallel to the first. They are now gently running in two parallel lines.

Each student puts a hand on the shoulder of the person running beside them and then the whole group moves forward again, hands on shoulders. This physical contact gets the group used to running in pairs, which is used in various other exercises and can always be used to establish a good communication with the partner.

NOTE: *Make sure students do not keep choosing the same person to run with in these exercises.*

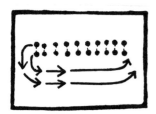

Once this pattern is established, the teacher asks the students to talk and to exchange greetings and to tell each other how they feel when they run. This continues for a few minutes. The teacher then asks the students to move their hands further across their partners' shoulders and run as closely as possible without disrupting the other. Then, as they are running, they move away from their partners until only the fingertips are touching. This is repeated as they run around the room.

The parallel lines of students are now asked to slow down and run on the spot. They are asked to drop their hands, losing contact with their partners and gently keep running on the spot.

The object now is to change partners and experience another rhythm. The front runner of one of the groups runs to the back of his/her line and the whole group moves forward one partner.

The exercise is repeated with as many partners as possible before the end of the session. Then go back to *the snake* and finish as usual.

Running Blind

◆

MANY SHALL RUN TO AND FRO,
KNOWLEDGE SHALL BE INCREASED.

DANIEL 12:4

This is a well known trust exercise adapted to running but, because the students run blind, safety must be observed.

The snake starts the exercise as it does each time. Once the group is used to running, two lines are formed and all put their hands on each other's shoulders (see Exercise 4). They break off as couples and run gently around the room. They can talk for a while to establish a rapport.

Then the couples run on the spot and are carefully told all about the exercise. One of the couple agrees to run with closed eyes and the other takes hold of the partner's arm and will be their 'eyes'. When all students are ready each couple moves off gently and slowly around the room. This goes on for five minutes and then, as the couples gain confidence, they can move faster. Some may even run quite quickly. Keep watching for safety.

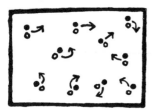

Now the couples are asked to slow down and run on the spot. The students who have their eyes closed are asked to keep them closed whatever happens. The 'seeing' students are then told to find a new partner and go to them and put their hands on their arm WITHOUT TALKING. The blind student should not know who the new partner is until the end of the exercise. When all students have a new partner, they then move forward again for a few minutes. This change-over is all done with the students running on the spot.

Now the students are asked to slow down and stop

WITHOUT OPENING THEIR EYES. The 'seeing' students still keep their hands on their partners. The blind students now tell their new partners what the difference was between them and their previous partners. When they have said their piece they are asked to open their eyes. They are still jogging.

Now the seeing students become blind and the whole exercise is repeated. The session ends with *the snake*.

Running Blind in Threes

THE RUNNER LIVES NEITHER IN THE PAST NOR IN THE FUTURE, BUT NOW, IN THE RUN.

DAVID E. CORBIN

This is a development of the previous exercise and again safety is a key factor. This can be a very liberating exercise if the students are given time to really gain trust.

The group starts off with *the snake* followed by the greeting exercise (see Exercise 3). Then running on the spot, then a quarter turn (90°) until all the students are facing sideways to the line like a chorus line of dancers. The teacher groups the students in threes, numbering from the leader, and each group of three put their hands on each other's shoulders. (If the numbers do not work out the teacher can take a place.) Then the groups of three run in random patterns around the

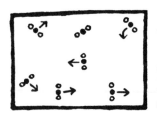

hall, hands still on shoulders. They can talk for a minute, establishing contact. They are then asked to run on the spot.

The student in the middle of the three closes his or her eyes and the two students on each side take hold of an arm. When all students are ready they start off slowly moving around the room. Because the student has two keepers he or she can become very confident. The object is for each person to run quickly with a feeling of complete confidence. To achieve really quick running, a one way system round the hall is preferred.

All are given a turn and *the snake* finishes off the session.

NOTE: *As these running blind exercises are repeated it becomes possible, with a great deal of care, to ask the student to run with his or her companion but not touching them, giving guidance by the voice only. This can be wonderful at a beach or open piece of ground where the students can run fast without danger.*

Two Lines Moving

◆

AND IN THE TIME OF THEIR
VISITATION THEY SHALL SHINE,
AND RUN TO AND FRO' LIKE
SPARKS AMONGST THE STUBBLE

THE WISDOM OF SOLOMON

The group starts off with *the snake* and runs gently round the room warming up. The teacher can introduce variations which relax various parts of the body at different times.

The group runs gently in line to the centre of the room and forms two parallel lines, each member of the class gently running on the spot next to a partner. Each pair puts hands on each other's shoulders and then the group moves into a trot around the room for a couple of minutes.

The leaders of the two lines peel off and run anywhere in the room they want. Be careful to start with, as a collision is quite possible at this stage.

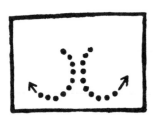

The lines should run in any random pattern for a while and then, when they feel confident, ask them to start to run in various ways which reflect the other line's movement. Let it develop if the patterns become interesting.

Then back to *the snake* to wind up in the usual way.

Shoulder to Shoulder

◆

To my amazement I saw fleeing through the early morning dusk a score of more or less naked youths, on each one a cow bell was dangling... Every young man was required to run ten, fifteen, twenty miles and even double this distance... as a matter of religion... They believed that since the air was the breath of the great spirit, to take more into their systems would automatically attune their minds and hearts more towards the great creative force they worshipped so reverently.

George James on the American Indian

The snake starts the day and when the group is warmed up they form two parallel lines and run with a partner for a few minutes. The runners who are leading each group then split off and each group runs as it will for a while.

Then the two groups slow down and run on the spot. They are asked to turn so they are now shoulder to shoulder in a row. At the signal they are asked to run slowly forward without colliding with the other group. (Hands on shoulders can be used to start to help keep in line.) They are told that if there is a danger of collision to run on the spot until the other group passes. It is important to emphasise that this exercise should be done slowly and that they should stay in line.

Each line is asked to revolve on its axis. The students in the

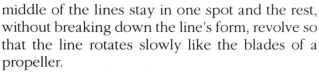

middle of the lines stay in one spot and the rest, without breaking down the line's form, revolve so that the line rotates slowly like the blades of a propeller.

One group is now asked to run to one end of the hall and jog on the spot facing into the space. The second group is asked to join onto the end of the first so that they are now one line again but running on the spot, shoulder to shoulder. They move forward in one line across the hall and then move backwards to their original position. This is done a few times but the students are asked to remember that they are still in fact two groups joined in the middle.

Then the line moves from one wall to the centre of the room and runs on the spot. Both groups, staying in line, start to rotate like a propeller in the same way as they have been practising in the two smaller groups – one clockwise and one anti-clockwise. The line will break in the middle and then come back together again facing the other direction.

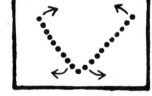

At the end of the exercise the two lines come back together and run for a while as *the snake* and slow down in the usual way.

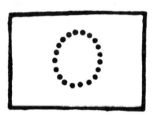

Sound and Movement

◆

**WHAT I'M TRYING TO DO IN RUNNING IS TO
REAFFIRM MY EXISTENCE.**

DON CHOI

After *the snake* warm-up, the group splits into two groups and they fall into parallel lines. They run for a while with hands on their partners' shoulders (see Exercise 4). The leader of each group now moves off, taking the group to run for a few minutes. The students are asked to remember their original partner.

The groups slow down and run on the spot, then make a quarter-turn until they are lined up shoulder to shoulder, and run forward slowly while still maintaining the line (see Exercise 6).

After they are established and moving in a line with confidence, one group goes to one end of the hall and runs on the spot and the second group goes to the other end. The students are now facing their original partners. In turn the students call out their partner's name – contact between each couple is forged down the length of the hall.

They slowly move towards each other keeping eye contact with their partner until they are a metre apart. Running gently backwards, they return to their respective ends of the hall.

The students call out to their partners using their names, every fourth beat. The groups go towards each other and the names get softer until they should only be a whisper when they are close. They increase in volume as they go back to the beginning. Alternatively, any words can be called and the students could make up calls and responses.

A further development of this exercise: the movement in Exercise 6, where the students move in a propeller-like motion, can be introduced into this exercise.

The two groups come towards each other down the hall and the calls diminish to a whisper. The groups are now facing each other. They start to wheel in a clockwise direction, the same distance apart, until they have changed places. The groups have now swapped ends of the hall.

Then back to *the snake* to wind up in the usual way.

River and Rocks

◆

THERE IS EVIDENCE THAT REGULAR AEROBIC EXERCISE INCREASES THE BLOOD LEVELS OF BETA-ENDORPHINS. BETA-ENDORPHINS ARE CHEMICALS THAT ARE PRODUCED IN THE BODY THAT ARE OFTEN DESCRIBED AS THE BODY'S OWN VERSION OF OPIATES... THESE CHEMICALS ARE SAID TO PRODUCE A FEELING OF WELL-BEING SOMETIMES REFERRED TO AS THE 'RUNNER'S HIGH'.

DAVID E. CORBIN

The exercise begins with *the snake* and continues for several minutes – this warms the students up and provides them with a 'gateway' though which they can pass from a normal state into work mode. Through repetition and habit they can start each session by relinquishing their thoughts in a ritual where the body begins to dictate their state of being.

The group breaks into four lines. The leaders are the first, sixth, the eleventh and the sixteenth members of the group and at a given signal they break away from the line and run where they will. Take care that there are no collisions.

The four groups can run at different paces and form temporary patterns against each other or run in tandem. At a pre-arranged signal the lines come back together in the original order. The groups fit together as smoothly as possible in a flowing movement.

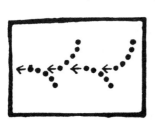

The group breaks up again and this manoeuvre is repeated.

The session finishes with *the snake*.

Sign of Infinity

◆

THE CENTIPEDE WAS HAPPY QUITE,
UNTIL THE TOAD IN FUN
SAID 'PRAY WHICH LEG GOES AFTER WHICH?'
AND WORKED HER MIND TO SUCH A PITCH,
SHE LAY DISTRACTED IN A DITCH
CONSIDERING HOW TO RUN.

MRS EDMUND CRASTER

This exercise is one of the most complex and helps greatly in the improvement of coordination and awareness.

The group warms up with *the snake* for several minutes and then gets into two lines as demonstrated in Exercise 4. Running in parallel lines, students establish a link with a partner, putting their hands on each other's shoulders.

Now, with hands off shoulders, both lines come into the middle of the room and gently run on the spot. The aim is for the two lines to cross through each other in the middle of the room making the sign for infinity – a figure-of-eight on its side. Each person has identified a partner and one side takes odd numbers and the other side even numbers.

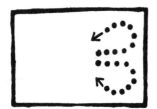

Each line runs down the centre of the hall to the end together. One team leader turns to the right and the other to the left and they run to the corners of the hall. They turn, but instead of running down the side of the hall they run diagonally across the hall very slowly, hardly moving forwards.

They now cross through each other, odd and even, odd and even, one after another, and on reaching the other corner turn and run down the side of the hall again.

This is repeated until the group is moving at normal speed. The group can keep turning and coming back into the middle in a continuous sign of infinity. A second crossing could even be added.

The snake is formed again and the runners come to a stop as usual.

NOTE: *This exercise takes some practice.*

Running and Flying

◆

WITH THE FIRST DREAM THAT COMES
WITH THE FIRST SLEEP
I RUN, I RUN,
I AM GATHERED TO THY HEART.

ALICE MEYNELL

This exercise involves carrying people and can be dangerous. Every care should be extended to the one who is being carried, particularly in lifting and putting down. The head should be looked after by one person.

The session starts with *the snake* and when the teacher feels that the group is well warmed up, it is divided into two in the usual way. One member from each group is asked to volunteer to be carried by the group. All students should have a chance to be carried during the session but no one should be forced.

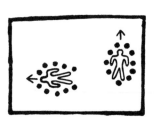

The volunteer lies down on the floor and relaxes completely, there should be no tension in the body. The members of the group pick up the volunteer carefully and place him or her on their shoulders, without letting go with their hands, and walk quietly around the room. When confidence has been built the group can begin to trot gently on the spot and, if it feels safe, move forward. Each student gets a turn for a time. A drum or music can be introduced. Lower each person gently and safely, taking particular care of the head.

The session finishes with *the snake*.

Drums, Music, Songs and Mantras

◆

This is another basic exercise which can open out into many areas and in fact can form the basis for a number of separate exercises. It involves running to sound and has four sections. I keep these sessions free and easy. Sometimes they have turned into a dance where the runners have started to move their bodies and feet to a dance beat. I let this evolve where it will. The main aim is to instil the joy of movement and its alliance with sound.

The teacher might keep returning to a music session every now and again to punctuate other exercises or use music inside some of the other sessions. This is a moveable feast.

The runners warm-up as usual, listening to the sound of their own feet.

THE DRUM

WE ARE FULL OF RHYTHMS – OUR PULSE, OUR GESTURES, OUR DIGESTIVE TRACTS, THE LUNAR AND SEASONAL CYCLES.

YEHUDI MENUHIN

Drums and percussion instruments relate closely to our inner beat – and it is to this form of sound that we turn first. One part of the group can sit out and play for the other and then they can swap roles. Alternatively the teacher or an outside person can provide a beat.

It is possible to experiment with all or some of the members of the group running with instruments, playing as they go, experimenting with different sounds and rhythms.

Recorded music also works as it gives you the range you might want with different types of drumming from all around the world. It can make a big difference to the run if, for example, you play African drums as opposed to Indian drums.

MUSIC

IF MUSIC BE THE FOOD OF LOVE PLAY ON.

WILLIAM SHAKESPEARE

Again this might be provided by some of the students or an outside source. Recorded music gives us the world of music from Mozart to Russian folk music. It is good to try as wide a range as possible and find what types of music are best for the group.

I believe that the whole group should like the music being regularly played as it is absorbed at a deep level and everyone should feel happy with the sound.

THE SONG AND THE HUMAN VOICE.

IF YOU CAN TALK, YOU CAN SING
IF YOU CAN WALK, YOU CAN DANCE.

AFRICAN SAYING

The first part of this exercise might be dedicated to recorded music where different types of songs can be demonstrated and the members of the group can centre on the sounds they like best. Then they can sing along.

Students can sing songs that they know and teach to the rest of the group as they move around. An individual might sing the verse and the group the chorus – or a call and response work song as sung by Black Americans. Clapping rhythms can be used with the songs.

A round or a four-part harmony can be learnt and the students who are singing each part can run together. The line can split up into separate running groups defined by the parts they sing.

Readings of various sorts are possible. These can include scripts.

THE MANTRA

CAROLLING FREE, SINGING OUR SONG TO GOD,
CHANTING OUR CHANT OF PLEASANT EXPLORATION.

WALT WHITMAN.

This is running to a sound or group of sounds made by the group as they run. It can be one word said in rhythm, such as the name of a toy (see Exercise 14) or the name of a bird (see

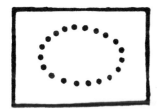

Exercise 23) or a word which everyone says at once. These words can be said out loud or internalised by each individual. The word can be substituted by a sound or grunt and can be uttered in unison or separately.

The breath can be used to utter sound or chant and again, can be done either individually, or as a prearranged sound with the whole group. Sound can be used as the breath comes in, or out, or both. This can be done quietly by every student or vocalised more loudly together. Call and response can be experimented with, and the single line can be split up in any combination of groups and sound.

Running Lives

◆

THE SOUND OF THE LEFT FOOT AS IT HITS THE GROUND IN CONSTANT RHYTHM... CONCENTRATE ON THIS SOUND: THE CHANGES IN IT, THE FULLNESS OF IT, THE CHARACTER OF IT. THINK ABOUT THE SOUND AS IT RINGS ON THE GROUND, THE SOUND OF EFFORT, OF HARMONY, OF RHYTHM, OF BEAUTY. THINK ABOUT THE INTERACTION OF THE FOOT WITH THE GROUND AND HOW THEY BECOME UNITED, THEN SEPARATED... THINK ABOUT HOW THAT SOUND NOT ONLY COMES FROM THE FOOT BUT ALSO FROM THE HEAD; OF UNITY BETWEEN FOOT(BODY) AND MIND; OF THE UNITY BETWEEN MIND, FOOT AND EARTH. CONCENTRATE ON THAT SOUND.

GERRY EGGER

This is the first of the exercises which is contemplative and thoughtful. I have found that it is better to intersperse the contemplative exercises with the more active ones than run them as a block. I have written an approximation of what *I* say but each teacher can adapt the exercise to whatever feels comfortable. The timing between each age is up to the teacher. The important thing is for the students to run quietly through their lives remembering what they will, getting a sense of the breadth of their years.

The snake starts off the session, and warm-up movements such as arm stretches and swivelling hips can be used to make the sure the runners are relaxed and well stretched.

The next section of this exercise is used EVERY time that a contemplative run is used.

The teacher asks the students to put the energy of the run into different parts of the body. The energy, the force to move forward, centres itself in the head, then it transfers to the neck, then chest and so on until it gets to the feet. Ask the students to note how the run changes as different parts of the body act as the centre of motivation. The pace and rhythm should not increase or decrease as the students do this. Now the teacher gets the students to transfer the energy of the run into the feet, finally reaching the earth – it is in this beat that the meditative power is found.

The teacher asks the group to keep up a steady rhythm and to relax. The direction is changed regularly but the leader remains the same. Allow the beat of the feet on the floor to really become established. The group should be now finding its own speed, breathing and timing.

The teacher is now going to run the class members through their lives. The students just keep running, listening to the voice...

> *We start as an egg floating in our own mother's womb and we start as a sperm swimming in our father. They come together and create you... Now you are growing in your mother's womb and it takes nine months. You are small to start with, your heart beating in twenty-four days, but as each month goes past you grow... Now you are born. You feel around you the tension as muscles force you down and suddenly into the outside world. Do you remember?... You open your eyes and are awake... Now you start your first year, you are aware of the world around you until you are talking and taking your first steps...*

With intervals I go slowly through each year of childhood. I ask questions which the students can call out in line or all together, such as a favourite toy or animal or favourite book or the names of their mum and dad. Then on to teenage life, school, a good teacher, the first kiss, a favourite song and then adulthood, each year being called out and time being left in each section for past experiences to be thought on. I go up to the age of the oldest member in the room.

The students then shake out the exercise and snake down to a stop. This session can end very quietly with some emotion (see Stamping Exercise 10).

PREPARATION: *This is to be prepared for Exercise 15. Each person should find a song that was a hit in the year of his or her birth and if possible learn to sing it. Also find a climactic event which took place in that year.*

Running the Years

◆

APPLAUD US WHEN WE RUN;
CONSOLE US WHEN WE FALL;
CHEER US WHEN WE RECOVER;
BUT LET US PASS ON.

EDMUND BURKE

This exercise is designed for fun and can be good for group dynamics.

The group warms up with *the snake* and then the youngest student runs to the front of the group. The second youngest runs to second place and so on until the line is running from the youngest to the oldest.

This continues for a while until the rhythm is again restored. Then the teacher asks the youngest student what year they were born, say, for example, it was 1975. The teacher then asks all the students born in that year to run together as a loose-knit group. Then the year of birth of the next youngest is investigated which is say 1972 and the students born in that year all run together. This goes on until each student is running with his or her own age group. They have a talk and exchange birthdays and so on. Some students run alone – I run up to them and listen to what they have to say.

Then the teacher asks the group to go back into line from the youngest to the oldest.

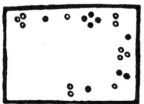

Students call out their birthdays and where they were born and the names of their parents.

Then going down the line again they call out what happened in that year, say the year of 1966, and also the songs that were popular then. Often some of the older students can remember the song and everyone can have a go at a couple of lines or even longer if possible.

The students then run around the room, relaxed and breathing easily. The teacher (who also has looked up some facts), starts to run through the years from the youngest age to the present day. Each year is marked with events and the songs and fashions and other data are mentioned. Again songs can be sung. A wonderful source of information for this exercise is *The Chronicle of the 20th Century,* published by Penguin Books and found in any public library. The last page of each year's section lists the hit songs.

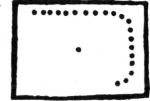

The group finish up with *the snake* slowing down to a stop (see Stamping Exercise 10).

NOTE: *For one reason or another some students might not want to give the information asked. This is fine and they can just join any group they want or run separately. This is made clear before the session starts.*

Running in a Spiral

◆

THE GENERATIONS OF LIVING THINGS PASS IN A SHORT TIME AND LIKE RUNNERS HAND ON THE TORCH OF LIFE.

LUCRETIUS

This exercise is designed for energy and coordination.

It starts as *a snake* but the object of the movement is an about-turn at a signal and to run in the opposite direction. The student at the back becomes the leader. So the signal might be the call 'one, two and turn' shouted in rhythm and the group immediately turns on the spot without breaking rhythm and runs in the opposite direction. When this has been perfected, the leader shouts out the call at random. The leaders are changed regularly.

Now that the group is working well with this exercise, the runners move in line into a spiral. The leader runs slowly around the room catching up with the tail, then runs past the tail on the inside – the spiral has started. It gets tighter and

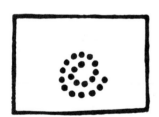

tighter until at the last moment the leader shouts the about-turn signal and the spiral unwinds itself. This movement sometimes requires a good deal of practice.

Then at the end of the exercise the spiral goes inward until it cannot go any further and stops. This is the end of the session.

Running the Body

◆

**SHINE BY THE SIDE OF EVERY PATH WE TREAD
WITH SUCH A LUSTRE, HE WHO RUNS MAY READ.**

WILLIAM COWPER

This is the second of the contemplative runs.

The group runs as *the snake* and relaxes, just getting into the rhythm, listening to the teacher's voice. The students transfer the source of running energy around their bodies and then into the run (see Exercise 14).

It starts with the description of the human skeleton, pausing from time to time to allow the runners to concentrate on each part. The whole exercise takes half an hour. This is how I do it:

I want you to concentrate on the bones inside your foot. They are working hard now, each moving against the next, carrying the weight of your body... How many can you identify?... What are your toes doing and what about your heel...

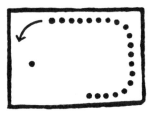

Next I talk them through the legs and into the hips. The journey continues up the spine, along the arms to the fingers, back up to the neck and into the head. I finish with the students imagining the whole skeleton working as one, running along.

I then move on to the muscles, tracing each set and feeling them working with the bones. Then on to the organs and feeling the heart doing its incredible job. I finish with the skin and the five senses – which completes the miracle of the running human body, each part working to propel us forward.

This can be adapted to examine how the body works in different expressions of movement such as starting to run or stopping or jumping and skipping.

I finish with *the snake* coming to a stop.

Entrance and Exit

◆

WRITE THE VISION, AND MAKE IT PLAIN

WRITE THE VISION, AND MAKE IT PLAIN
UPON TABLES, THAT HE MAY RUN THAT READETH IT.

HABAKKUK 2:2

This exercise is a useful theatre exercise and I developed it to teach students about running as an entrance and exit or as a tool in other theatre situations.

The group starts with *the snake* and runs for a few minutes developing rhythm and pace.

Runner number eleven leads off those behind to run as a separate group. They run up until they are parallel with the first group and put their hands on their partners' shoulders. They run like that for a while and then break off and run independently, remembering their partner.

One group lines up across one end of the hall, quarter turns and runs on the spot, shoulder to shoulder, facing down the hall. That group then remain as observers, gently jogging, watching the others, and they are asked to mentally note how these different entrances and exits work dramatically and why.

The other group lines up at the other end. The runners quarter turn until they are shoulder to shoulder facing the other group.

At a signal they all run in a line down the hall very slowly until they are within a metre of the other group. They then about-turn and run slowly back. The line then repeats this exercise but instead of turning runs backwards to the original positions.

Next, choose a word or phrase to repeat together, perhaps, 'Get out' or 'Weaving spiders come not here' and move forward chanting it and then retreat. The sounds can increase in volume or decrease. The students could also learn some lines from a script and try this exercise.

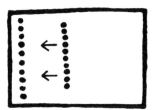

Then one at a time the runners come down the hall as fast as they can run and shout a word. As soon as one has finished, the next runs down until they have all had a turn. Variations on this action can be experimented with.

The students who have been working now become the spectators and *vice versa*.

The group is asked to run around the hall as one group. They keep close together and different group entrances can be attempted. The rioting crowd, the witnesses at a burning, protesters or a battle, are all useful to use and it is always interesting to include sound. The running rhythm is always in place.

Always running, individuals or smaller groups can run separately, experimenting with the dynamic of interacting with the big group. Script can be used, or simple cry and response.

As a final exercise the students run separately around the hall (start very slowly and watch for collisions). They are then asked, at a signal, to run to a spot anywhere in the hall and shout 'Yes' or any word, phrase or sentence that would seem useful and as soon as they have finished, run to another part and shout the same cry and then to a third place. They are not to touch anyone else. This helps develop random movement on stage.

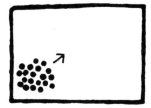

Each teacher and group can use any variation of these exercises to help build up awareness of running on stage and group movement.

The snake finishes off the session in the usual way.

Running the Hunt

◆

TARAHUMARA HUNTERS CAN LITERALLY RUN THE DEER THEY ARE TRACKING INTO THE GROUND. ONCE THEY DISCOVER AN ANIMAL'S TRACKS, SEVERAL MEN WILL COMMENCE TO JOG AFTER IT FOR MANY MILES, RARELY LOSING SIGHT OF THEIR INTENDED PREY. BY THE SECOND DAY OF STEADY METHODICAL CHASING, THE DEER USUALLY DROPS FROM SHEER EXHAUSTION, AND THE HUNTERS IMMEDIATELY POUNCE ON IT WITH KNIVES OR ROCKS.

NATURAL HISTORY, VOL.81

Members of the group warm up with *the snake* but they are asked to run on the sides of their feet, on the heels of their feet and on the toes of their feet and asked to note the difference. They are then asked to run as heavily as possible, really listening to the sound as their feet pound the floor. (Take care that students are not over enthusiastic – they could hurt themselves). Then they can run lightly, without sound and try to feel what they are doing differently in their bodies to cause this. Repeat the exercise a few times.

Next, they should run as if they are pursuing an animal and try to adopt a loping run, like a wolf, that can be sustained all day. Ask them to note what it is they are doing differently from normal. Run for a while.

Then, slowing down to running on the spot, they gather into a random circle. This is what I say:

> *You must make no noise, the game is near. You must become alert, your survival depends on your ability to run quickly and well. Run soundlessly as one group. The animal is eating grass on the other side of the room. You must approach without being heard. You must get near enough to be able to throw a spear.*

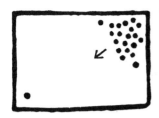

They approach, balanced, silent and when the signal is made they throw their spears. I ask, 'Have you frightened the game? If so try again.'

They go through the exercise a number of times. One or two of the group can become the animals, running when they hear anything – forcing the 'hunting' group to start again.

Then it's back to *the snake*. Shake out the exercise by shaking the body – then the usual slow down and stop.

Running Women and Men

◆

THE RUN. HERE THE INDIVIDUAL BECOMES AIRBORNE AND THE WHOLE SEQUENCE OF STRIDING CHANGES. THERE IS NO LONGER A MOMENT WHEN BOTH FEET ARE ON THE GROUND AT THE SAME TIME, BUT INSTEAD THERE IS A MOMENT WHEN BOTH FEET ARE OFF THE GROUND TOGETHER AND THE RUNNER IS 'SAILING THROUGH THE AIR'

DESMOND MORRIS

This is a simple exercise but in some ways a difficult one – it can produce a competitive atmosphere and can even be divisive.

The exercise starts as usual until the warm-up is completed. The women and the men form different groups and run in line. Once these have been established then random running can occur and the two groups can interrelate if it is appropriate.

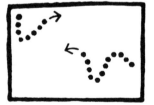

They then break up the line and start to run in a group forming various patterns as they go. Let each group notice the difference in the other.

The two groups come back together and run as a large group merging again. They then form a running line and slow to a stop.

Running Evolution

◆

DANCERS WEAR AND USE WHISTLES MADE OF THE
WING BONE OF THE EAGLE TO WHICH EAGLE PLUMES
ARE ATTACHED. IN RECREATING THE CRY OF THE
EAGLE, TO THE POWERFUL RHYTHM OF SONG, DANCE
AND DRUM, THE EAGLE IS EVER PRESENT IN THE VOICE
AND BEING, MAN'S VITAL BREATH IS UNITED WITH THE
ESSENCES OF SUN AND LIFE.

JOSEPH EPES BROWN

The third of the contemplative runs. After *the snake* warms everyone up, the energy is transferred into the foot gently hitting the floor (see Exercise 14).

As in the other meditative runs the students simply run around the room, changing direction every now and then, listening to the teacher's voice. The beat of the foot can change as the session moves through various stages. They can 'run' their thoughts into the floor.

The teacher takes the group back to the cosmos, long before the earth was formed. We feel a sun explode and the planets form. Each planet comes into existence until earth is reached. The teacher starts three billion years ago, describes the world and slowly traces the development of the planet through the eons, until life first appears.

The story moves from the smallest cells into the fish and first land animals. The dinosaurs come and go, then the birds and larger animals, and eventually the apes. The students then hear about the emergence of human beings and their evolution and the formation of states and nations, the lives of prophets, the rise and fall of empires, until we move into the 20th century. The years go past with major events until we move into the morning of the run.

The class finishes in the normal way. The more work the teacher does on this the more amazing the run can get.

A useful reference book is *The Chronicle of the World*, published by Penguin Books and found at any public library.

Music or drums can be used with this exercise.

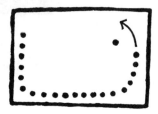

Running with Emotions

◆

BUT I, I CANNOT READ IT
(ALTHOUGH I RUN AND RUN)
OF THEM THAT DO NOT HAVE THE FAITH,
AND WILL NOT HAVE THE FUN.

G.K. CHESTERTON

The fourth of the contemplative runs.

This is a short, simple exercise to identify where the energy lies in the body when we feel a particular emotion. There is no correct answer to be found in this exercise and each student should think it through individually. It can help when playing certain parts in a theatre piece.

The group starts with *the snake* and then the teacher asks that the energy motivating the run move into the head, then the neck and so on around the body, ending with the feet.

Then the teacher tells the group to run with anger, maintaining ordinary pace but allowing the energy of this emotion to inhabit the body without strain and trouble, letting it come and go as the individual feels is necessary. Give the runners clear instructions to keep their feelings general and not to become upset about a real problem. This is a warm-up and the feelings should remain light. It is an exercise and should in no way become mentally distressing. As the students run, the following questions can be asked and if appropriate the students can reply.

Does it bring energy into any particular part of the body?
Does it alter the breathing?
Does it alter the run?

Then the teacher asks the students to 'shake' the emotions out of their system and then go back to normal running for a while.

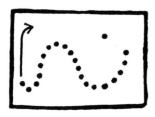

When the class has released that emotion the teacher can move on to joy, happiness, hate, loss etc. Watch carefully that the students are able to handle the emotions that ensue. If problems seem to be arising, move on to another exercise.

The group finish with *the snake*, coming to a stop together, as usual.

Running the Birds

◆

THEY SHALL MOUNT UP LIKE EAGLES; THEY SHALL
RUN AND NOT BE WEARY;
THEY SHALL WALK AND NOT FAINT.

ISAIAH 40: 31

The fifth of the contemplative runs.

Although I start with birds, this run is designed to get the students to focus on their relationships with other creatures on the planet. Again, as with the other contemplative runs, the students do not pretend to be these animals but attempt to feel their spirit, their nature if you like, their rhythm as they run.

Start with *the snake* until everyone is warmed up and running smoothly. Note how the group has changed in its expressiveness since Exercise 1. The energy is passed around the body and then into the run as in Exercise 14.

As the group runs the teacher begins to describe the sensations of flight in its different forms. The birds that soar, the ones that hunt, the migratory birds that cover huge distances, the birds that move their wings slowly, the ones that flap quickly to sustain themselves in the air. Slowly leaving gaps for thought, the group is taken through the different kinds of birds, for example, eagles, sparrows, emus, humming birds, pelicans, swallows, hawks and cranes, with the leader changing each time a different bird is mentioned.

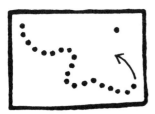

The snake finishes this exercise. Other animals and insects can be used in the same way. I have had classes that spontaneously lifted their arms and simulated flight. When this happened I developed it, but it is not an essential part of the session.

Food

◆

MARATHON RUNNING IS AN ART FORM AS DEMANDING AS ANY OTHER. THE MOTIVATIONS RUN DEEP, THE RUNNING ITSELF IS TOO SPECIAL AND DREAMLIKE TO EVER BE COMPLETELY MINED.

JIM SHAPIRO

This, the sixth contemplative run, is designed to run through thoughts and meditate on areas of nourishment. It is run quietly and in a relaxed way.

It starts with *the snake* and runs to the voice of the teacher. See Exercise 14 for the first part of the exercise, as the energy is passed around the body and into the feet.

'We follow the life of the world.' I generally proceed to describe space and where we are in it, slowly centring into our part of the cosmos and to the earth moving around the sun. Then I move the minds of the group through the atmosphere and around the world, as if in a rocket looking down on the seas, the mountains and the deserts. At each stage I leave pauses for the students to fill with their own thoughts.

'Then down onto earth and into a market garden. It has a high wall and it grows fruit and vegetables.' I describe the place physically and move around the garden looking at the plants. The apple and pear trees, the tomatoes and beans and the potatoes and leeks. I describe the texture and the smell, the birds and the animals and the insects that help the process and the rain and sun and the earth that make it all possible.

I move to the fields with the crops growing and to the harvest.

And then to the kitchen, where I prepare a fresh salad with the bread baking in the oven and the vegetables being prepared (especially those Greek olives), then sit in the garden and eat.

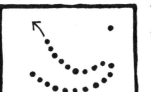

Then back to *the snake* and finish. (For some reason the group always wants to stop here to eat lunch!)

Running the Name

◆

WHAT'S IN A NAME?

WILLIAM SHAKESPEARE

A simple exercise if the class is in a hurry.

It starts with running *the snake* until everyone is warmed up. Then the leader runs across the hall running out their name as if writing it on the floor, saying each letter as they run. The others follow calling out the letter they are on. The leader must spell the name in one length of the hall. Every one gets a turn and the session finishes with writing 'THE END' and coming to a stop as usual.

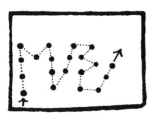

Tunnel of Joy

◆

RUNNING BRINGS HEALTH AND JOY. IT IS LIKE AIR, LIKE THE EARTH.

MIKI GORMAN.

This is an exercise that I use if the group needs a real lift, something that will shake everyone up and let them enjoy themselves.

The snake as usual to start and then into three groups who run randomly around the hall. When they feel good with one another, the first group runs to a corner of the hall and the other two to the diametrically opposite corner. The leader of the single group leads the line towards the centre of the room, and towards the opposite corner. At the same time the other two groups make a similar move, running in parallel, about a metre apart, towards the approaching single group.

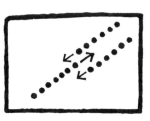

Very slowly the two parts of the class run towards each other until the single group runs through the middle corridor created by the double group. This is repeated a few times and it gets faster until everyone is confident.

Now sound is introduced and as the single group runs through, the other two groups shout loudly. It's like passing through a tunnel.

Now the runners touch open palms as they pass through or duck under the raised hands of the other groups as in certain dances.

Each group gets a turn and the session is ended with *the snake* coming to a stop.

The Elements and the Seasons

◆

TO REACH THE INNER BEAT, THE HEART BEAT, THE
EARTH BEAT.

DAVID E. CORBIN

The seventh contemplative run.

This is a simple exercise which allows experimentation with different rhythms. This is a meditative run – the students do not to try to emulate the various elements, but only feel their energy as they run. In doing so, does the rhythm change?

The exercise starts with *the snake* and uses the technique employed in Exercise 14 to transfer energy into the run. Breaking into four groups, each takes one of the elements – earth, fire, water or air – and runs with this feeling. Interaction can occur and should be allowed to develop.

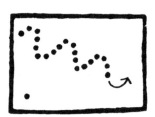

It is the same with the four seasons. Each group takes the spirit of one of the seasons and runs with summer, autumn, winter or spring. The teacher can talk about each season and changes in response to weather.

Finish with *the snake* coming to a stop.

NOTE: *This exercise can be done to music which can be used with, or even replace, the teacher's voice.*

Running Rivers to the Sea

◆

THE GREAT SEA
MOVES ME!
THE GREAT SEA
SETS ME ADRIFT!
IT MOVES ME
LIKE ALGAE ON STONES
IN RUNNING BROOK WATER.
THE VAULT OF HEAVEN
MOVES ME!
THE MIGHTY WEATHER
STORMS THROUGH MY SOUL.
IT TEARS ME WITH IT
AND I TREMBLE WITH JOY.

BOOK OF ESKIMOS **BY PETER FREUCHENS**

The eighth, and last, contemplative run.

This is an exercise which follows the journey of the water as it turns from rain to river water and goes to the sea and then back to rain again.

The group starts the run with *the snake*, relaxed and breathing easily. As in all the other contemplative exercises the energy is passed around the body and ends up in the rhythm of the run.

The teacher asks everyone to concentrate on the energy of what is being said. Again, the text can vary from person to person.

'We start at the bottom of the sea, deep in the cold water, strange fish, black rhythms, then the water slowly heats and comes to the surface.' The teacher follows the moisture as it evaporates into the sky and becomes cloud, moving in the wind building up to rain. Lightning and thunder rip through and the water falls as rain into the mountain streams. The small stream tumbles down the valleys, gathering strength, falls as waterfalls and swirls as deep pools and becomes a wide meandering river filled with life, eventually coming through the delta to the sea.

The session finishes off with *the snake* coming to a stop at the bottom of the sea again. This exercise can be done to music.

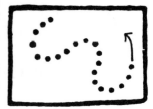

NOTE: *These contemplative runs can be useful when a dramatic piece needs to be explored. The director or teacher can talk through the story, ideas and themes that the performers might be working on. The performers have a chance to visualise as they run.*

Star Signs

◆

RUNNING TEACHES THE VALUE OF DILIGENCE, HARD
WORK, COURAGE, MUTUAL RESPECT AND HONESTY...
AND YOU DON'T HAVE TO WEAR A TIE.

SAMUEL SCHUMAN

This is one of the last exercises and can be revealing.

Start as *the snake* and warm up. Anyone who is the sign of
Aquarius is asked to run in the front. Next comes Pisces who
form a group and run behind Aquarius. And so it goes on until
there are twelve groups running around the hall. If one sign is
missing then leave a gap.

They run around talking about their common characters,
and then the teacher asks them to fall into line but to stay in
their star order. Then, still running, they come into
a circle and run on the spot.

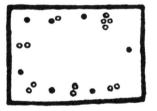

Each star sign group then enters the ring in turn
and the rest call out what they see as similar
characteristics within the group. As the last group
go out to their places again the students gradually
slow down until they all stop at the same time.

PREPARATION: *At the end of the session students are asked to
find their Chinese astrological sign, which can be run the
next day.*

Running Without Running

◆

'THERE WILL BE A NEW DANCE,' SHE CALLED OUT. 'A LAUGHING DANCE.'

SHE TAUGHT THE PEOPLE THAT WHILE THIS LAUGHING SONG WAS SUNG EVERY ONE HAD TO BE VERY SOLEMN. THERE SHOULD BE NO SMILES, NO SIGN OF JOY...

THE PEOPLE BEGAN TO DANCE... WAITING FOR THE STOPS IN THE SONG – THEN RUNNING OUT, POINTING TO ELDERS AND LAUGHING IN THEIR MANY VOICES. WHEN THE SONG WOULD BEGIN AGAIN, THEY WOULD RETURN TO THEIR CIRCLE DANCING, TRYING TO LOOK SOLEMN, BUT EACH OF THEIR FACES WOULD BREAK OUT INTO A SMILE.

AND THIS WAS THE WAY OF IT, WE SOMETIMES END WITH THE LAUGHING SONG, SO ALL WILL GO HOME WITHOUT JEALOUSY OR ANGRY HEARTS. IT IS THE ONLY TIME IN OUR LIFE WE MAKE FUN OF THE OLD PEOPLE... THE OLD PEOPLE THINK IT'S THE FUNNIEST OF ALL.

INDIAN TALE RETOLD BY TERRY TAFO

This is the final exercise when a group is about to break up. It starts as usual with *the snake*. By now the group should be feeling fit and well. The pace, strength and coordination will have all improved. So in this last run the teacher should let the runners really stretch and feel the joy of their bodies.

They slow down and stop in the usual way and then walk to a part of the room where they feel comfortable and stand and shut their eyes. Let them consider their breathing and their body in repose. Let them think about what their bodies do when running and imagine in their minds that they are moving forward.

The students are asked to open their eyes when tapped on the shoulder. The first is tapped on the shoulder and then led to the front to look at the faces of all the others. The teacher takes the student back and another student is tapped and led to the front, and so on through the group.

Finally, ask the students to open their eyes, say loudly the first word that comes into their heads and go on a last *snake,* coming to a stop as usual and then say goodbye.

Remember, all these running exercises can be repeated outside on the grass, or any suitable open space.

PART THREE

The Stamping

HERE AM I, BEHOLD ME
I AM THE SUN
BEHOLD ME.

LAKOTA SUNRISE GREETING SONG

The first time I saw Aboriginal dancing in the natural environment I was amazed. Here was a chance to watch people from one of the oldest living cultures in the world and to watch a dance which had been handed down through many generations. The dancers were all male and mostly older men and younger boys. They wore red cloth around their waists and their bodies were painted all over with white and yellow ochre. The only sound was the crackle of the camp fire and the corroboree sticks clicking. Some of the older men wore tall woven conical head gear in yellow and black with white feathers woven through.

The dancers formed a line and the songs began, chanted and continuously sung low in the throat, full of power.

Each man would gently stamp on the ground and before long the red dust rose up in clouds. Every now and again one of the dancers would come forward as the song began and stamp powerfully on the ground with such intensity that it seemed as if the ground was vibrating.

It was very impressive and I thought that I might try to develop my running exercises into stamping. I did not want to mimic the sacred dances of the aboriginal people in any way, but wanted to allow students to learn the power that their movement communicated.

Introduction to the Stamping Exercises

◆

THE DANCERS MOVED IN A CIRCLE WITH CLAPPED
HANDS AND SLOW DRAGGING STEPS, SINGING WITH
RHYTHMIC SWING THE SONGS OF THE SPIRIT-DANCE.
ROUND AND ROUND WENT THE CIRCLE, WHILE EVERY
NOW AND THEN A DANCER STAGGERED FROM THE RING
AND FELL SWOONING IN A TRANCE. ON 'AWAKENING'
THE 'DREAMER' DESCRIBED HIS VISION OF THE SPIRITS'
WORLD. THE EXPERIENCE OF THE TRANCE WAS
EMBODIED IN THE SPONTANEOUS SONG, TO BE
THEREAFTER USED IN THE DANCE.

PETER NABOKOV

AIMS

The stamping exercises have been developed to bring the running exercises down to earth, to alter that sense of flying through the air and to transfer the energy right down through the body to the feet and then to the earth. Tadashi Suzuki, the Japanese theatre director said:

> *The gesture of stamping on the ground, whether performed by Europeans or Japanese, gives the actor a sense of the strength inherent in his own body. It is a gesture that can lead to the creation of a fictional space, perhaps even a ritual space, in which the actor's own body can achieve a transformation from the personal to the universal.*

For dynamic physical theatre, Western actors need to take their energy out of their heads and put it in their bodies. So often actors keep the energy of their movement in the head, shoulders and arms – it is cerebral and word orientated. Stamping exercises help move expression throughout the body. They reduce conscious thought and increase the whole body's ability to express and communicate.

The exercises are difficult at first and students often fight to keep their energy in their heads, not wanting the mind to lose control, not wanting to relinquish the mental for the physical. They are happy to use voice, face, hands and arms to express themselves, but they fear the release of primal energy. However, with practice these exercises start to move the energy from the head down into the body and they start to push energy into the feet. After a time this transfer of energy can have a profound effect on the actor's performance.

Many of the exercises are the same as the running ones – this is intentional. It is easier if the exercise is familiar so that the process can be forgotten and concentration is on the transfer of energy.

Before starting these exercises there is a very important safety comment. Running is a natural activity – we are designed to run – but stamping is not. Hitting the floor with the flat of the foot can be very dangerous if it is done too hard or for too long.

I recommend that the teacher runs the running classes for some weeks before moving on to stamping. All teachers should remain extremely vigilant when students stamp on a wooden floor. *Concrete floors are unsuitable for these exercises.*

I have put a notional exercise time at the top of each exercise but there are no hard-and-fast rules. The sessions should last as long as the teacher finds useful and safe.

The teacher should switch to the stamping exercises for only a few minutes a day as part of the appropriate running classes and warn the students to stamp LIGHTLY. The students should stamp slowly and gently, putting the whole foot down at once. It is better to get this right than to increase speed and become sloppy.

Ian Curruthers said of Suzuki's work:

The stronger the stamping, the more the energy generated – but the harder it is to maintain control. The actor must try to prevent the stamping from producing 'shake' or 'wobble' in the upper body, which looks weak. This can be done by learning to 'block' or control this energy in the area between the hips (the actor's centre of gravity) which must remain firm in all situations if the body is to be truly expressive.

And in Suzuki's own words:

The feet have provided, up until now, the ultimate means of connection between man and earth.

TECHNIQUE

Students are asked to bend their knees slightly before beginning. Raise the knee in front of the body and bring the foot down flat on the floor.

It is important that heel and toe strike the floor at the same time. It is not important that the floor is struck hard, only that the foot is flat as it hits the floor.

NOTE: *Many people raise the foot behind them, leaving the knee in its usual position. This is not correct. The leg should be raised forwards from the hip, bent at the knee. Start the exercises slowly, making sure this technique is mastered before speed and intensity are increased.*

Stamping
A 10-Minute Exercise

This is a short introduction to stamping which the students can begin at the end of a running session.

After running around the hall in *the snake* they are asked to slow down and run in one line, on the spot, along the length of the room, then to do a quarter-turn and run on the spot shoulder to shoulder.

The teacher asks the group to keep running on the spot but to slow down the running to a very slow pace, then to SLOWLY and GENTLY change from landing on the toes, with heels following, to landing with the whole foot on the ground. They are now stamping and should practice going from running to stamping and back again.

The students then close their eyes and concentrate on the energy source and where it is coming from in their bodies, then open their eyes again.

More stamping and then they are asked to move the motivation for the stamping to the feet. The energy should be in the legs and soles of the feet. Let them experiment with this for a while. The teacher can go to the aid of individuals who are having trouble.

After they have got the idea, they move across the room keeping in line and then move backwards to their original position. This should be repeated a few times.

The students then go back to running whichever exercise they were doing.

This exercise can be included in the running sessions for a few days.

Stamping the Line
A 10-Minute Exercise

◆

The runners come down to running on the spot along the length of one side of the hall and quarter-turn until they are shoulder to shoulder.

Now they transfer the running into gentle stamping and move in line across the room and back again, keeping in a straight line. This is repeated a couple of times. Then sound is introduced.

They all say a word and repeat it in time with the stamping (at an interval the teacher deems appropriate) and move across the hall increasing the volume of the word. As they stamp backwards to their original positions their voices should diminish to a whisper. Keep the energy in the lower body and repeat, experimenting with the length of the vocalisation and volume of the voice.

Then back to a running exercise.

Stamping in Two Groups
A 15-Minute Exercise

◆

The runners break off into two groups of ten in the usual way and then line up shoulder to shoulder at opposite ends of the hall, facing each other and running on the spot.

They are asked to transfer from running to stamping gently on the floor, concentrating their energy in the legs and feet. At a signal they approach each other down the hall until they are a couple of metres apart and then they go back to the ends of the room. This is repeated a couple of times and on the last time they greet each other when they meet in the middle.

Then each group is given a word to repeat in time with the stamping. The words can be opposites such as 'give' and 'take' or complementary such as 'truth' and 'beauty'. The two groups come up the hall again chanting the words alternately and then move back to the ends again. Once more they come up the hall and the volume of the words increases and diminishes.

Now that they have something to say there is a tendency to begin thinking, but they should keep concentrating on the stamping – the body.

Then back to running.

The Sun and the Moon

A 10-Minute Exercise

The runners make two lines running on the spot and put their hands on each other's shoulders. The teacher asks them to transfer from running to stamping and gently stamp out a rhythm with their partner. Once this is established they start running on the spot again and separate.

The two groups line up facing each other at each end of the hall as in the previous exercise and move from running to stamping.

One group becomes the sun and the other the moon. The sun group of runners moves forward in line down the hall until they are all in the middle and then move backwards to their original positions. Then it is the turn of the moon to do the same.

They repeat the exercise but this time they make sound, going from a gentle sound as they start, to a loud sound in the middle, and as they return backwards, the sound again diminishes.

Now concentrate the attention on 'stamping' the energy of the sun or the moon into the floor. Do not do this too violently. When the energy has really transferred into the legs and feet, move forward and repeat the exercise. We see the sun 'rising' to its full power and setting again and likewise with the waxing and waning of the moon.

Now both groups move in towards the centre until they are a couple of metres from one another and then back to the ends of the room.

As confidence is gained, when the two groups have reached the middle, they can slowly wheel round as one line until they have changed places, and then back to the start.

Then back to the running exercise.

PREPARATION: *This is to be prepared by the students for Exercise 7. The students have to come into class with the name of a wild animal. They must have seen this creature between now and the time set for Exercise 7 and it is important that they have not mechanically chosen this animal but that the animal has attracted their attention – chosen them, as it were. It can be an insect, a bird, a creature of any sort, as long as it is not domesticated.*

Male and Female

A 15-Minute Exercise

The runners split into two groups as usual and come to face each other from the ends of the hall as in the previous exercise.

The runners are asked to move from running to stamping gently, concentrating on the energy being in the beat that the feet make on the ground.

One group is allocated to be the male energy and the other the female energy. This is not the energy of human beings but of all life. They then work together to work out a stamp that reflects these forces. Each might be different.

They then come down the hall in a line keeping to their own rhythm, until they are a couple of metres apart. They then move back. The next time sound can be introduced.

Once the group members feel comfortable in the rhythm they are asked to break up their line and form a random group, but not to lose their beat.

The two groups now move around the hall at will. They can interrelate with the other group or not, as the case may be.

Then, back to running.

NOTE: *At all times during these longer stamping exercises the group can be asked to run for a while if they are losing concentration or getting tired. But it is important not to allow them to stop to rest and thereby lose rhythm – this completely breaks up the exercise.*

Music and Sound

This exercise can be used in concert with Running Exercise 13 and the same basic principles apply.

All stamping exercises can use sound in any form. Pre-recorded music can be played and all styles of music can be used. The group can also use percussion instruments as they move through the exercises which, in harmony with the stamping beat, can create very exciting rhythms.

But stamping can also produce its own rhythm unaided by other instruments. The stamping feet produce a beat, and with different groups developing different rhythms the results can be full of energy and life. They can also be interspersed with clapping.

Then, back to running.

Animal

A 20-Minute Exercise

◆

The runners slow down and run on the spot. Moving slowly forward until they form a large circle, they then turn until they are facing the centre. They change from running to stamping lightly on the floor and must concentrate their energy into the stamping.

When a rhythm has been successfully established they tune in to each other and continue stamping. Going around the circle each student in turn enters the circle and stamps on the floor with the rhythm of the animal which has attracted them (see PREPARATION at the end of Exercise 4). They in *no* way try to imitate the animal's movements but merely stamp its feeling or spirit.

The students can play music or percussion to this, adjusting the sound to each animal. Then the teacher asks one person to repeat and this time another student can enter and they can stamp with each other. This can build to a number of students being in the circle.

Then, back to normal running.

The Parent and Child
A 5-Minute Exercise

◆

The runners split into two groups facing each other from either end of the hall. They are running shoulder to shoulder with arms on each other's shoulders. The running is changed to gentle stamping.

One group moves down the hall in a single line to within two metres of the other group and slowly retreats. Then the other group has a turn.

One group is selected as the parent and the other as the child. They work until the rhythm suits them. These beats might be different.

The parent group comes up the hall and introduces the word 'child', which is repeated at each convenient beat, then the group moves back again. The child group then does the same thing but uses the word 'mother' or 'father'. Do not start to act characters but just stamp the energy.

Now the two groups approach each other, chanting the chosen words and meeting in the middle of the room. They then go back to the start. This is practised a few times. Volume and rhythm can be experimented with.

All then come to the middle of the room and the two groups put out their hands, keeping the energy low in the body – they touch hands. At this point the stamping of the two groups might have united in the one rhythm, which is fine.

The other parent role can now be used.

The teacher finishes the exercise here and the students go back to running.

NOTE: *The identities and word chosen can be changed at will and the exercise can be used again and again experimenting with different group identities. They can be aggressive towards each other, loving, or neutral but as each identity is chosen ask the students to note the change in the stamping.*

As an Acting Tool

◆

This is a good exercise to develop stage craft and links well with Running Exercise 18. It can last as long as the teacher thinks is useful.

The runners form two groups running in parallel lines and then come slowly to a stop, running on the spot. One group then runs to one end of the hall and round on a quarter-turn, shoulder-to-shoulder facing down the hall.

The other group members come around a quarter turn, putting hands on each other's shoulders. Then, transferring to the stamping movement they keep the energy in the feet. They lower their arms.

The teacher asks them to move across the hall as if they are coming on stage and to put the energy of that entrance into the feet. The same movements are used with exits. The students can develop many different ways of doing this. There should be no attempt to act but rather to generate a certain type of energy. The other group then has a turn.

Now the first group goes back to stamping and each individual student comes forward across the floor in any pattern, practising putting energy into the feet, but now characters can emerge. There is no attempt at realism but more the act of stamping the 'energy' of the character into the ground. Small groups can now stamp forwards taking on character and this can even work up to the whole group. By this time it should be easier to tell when the student's energy starts to leave the body and go back to the mind. Whenever this happens, move the energy back to the feet.

The group go back to running.

Self

A 5-Minute Exercise

◆

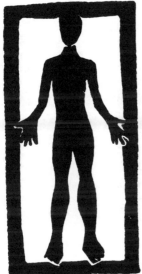

This exercise integrates well with Running Exercises 14 and 15.

The runners slow down to running on the spot. They then move apart slowly until they find a spot of their own. The teacher asks them to transfer from running to stamping and to close their eyes.

When they are gently stamping on the spot they are asked to 'stamp' their lives into the earth – to spend five minutes going slowly through their lives and transferring those thoughts to the ground. Again, make sure the students avoid straining themselves physically.

Then the group goes back to running.

THE SUN DANCE, THUS, IS NOT A CELEBRATION BY MAN FOR MAN; IT IS AN HONOURING OF ALL LIFE AND THE SOURCE OF ALL LIFE, THAT LIFE MAY GO ON, THAT THE CYCLE BE A CYCLE, THAT ALL THE WORLD AND MAN MAY CONTINUE ON THE PATH OF THE CYCLE OF GIVING, RECEIVING...

JOSEPH EPES BROWN

Up early in Port Douglas some years ago I drove to the beach. It was deserted and I stripped off and began to run along the firm sand that separates water from shore. The sea splashed as the soles of my feet hit the ground. The sea sparkled and the birds called. It was a lovely morning and I sank into a sort of thoughtless state. I was suddenly aware that I was not alone. I looked up and there was no one to be seen in any direction. I looked out to sea and there, not thirty metres out, were three dolphins swimming along parallel to me. I could swear that they were keeping pace and 'running' with me. I slowed down and sure enough they slowed down too. I thought I must be dreaming. I speeded up and they swam faster, quite able to follow the path of an earth-bound human. We ran in concert together until I got to the end of the beach. I turned around and began to come back. They were on some other journey and swam out to sea. I stood knee-deep in the water and bade them goodbye.

Neil Cameron, Maleny, January 1995

LET US LAY ASIDE EVERY WEIGHT, AND THE SIN WHICH
DOTH SO EASILY BESET US, AND LET US RUN WITH
PATIENCE THE RACE THAT IS SET BEFORE US.

HEBREWS 12:1

Select Bibliography

◆

On the Road: The Marathon, Jim Shapiro, Crown Publishing, New York.

Running High, Garry Egger, Sun Publishing, Santa Fe.

Jogging, David E. Corbin, HarperCollins, Sydney, 1987.

The Indian Book, Natalie Curtis, Dover Publications, New York.

Spiritual Wisdom of the Native Americans , John Heinerman, Cassandra Press, San Rafael, 1989.

The Indians of the Great American Plains , Bancroft-Hunt and Forman

I Become Part of It, D.M. Dooling and Paul Jordan-Smith (Ed.), HarperCollins

Manwatching, Desmond Morris, Triad, London, 1978.

Book of Eskimos, Peter Freuchens, Fawcett

The Way of Acting, Tadashi Suzuki, Theatre Communication Group, New York, 1986.

First published in 1995 by
Currency Press Ltd,
PO Box 452, Paddington,
NSW 2021, Australia

Published simultaneously in the USA by Heinemann
A Division or Reed Publishing (USA) Inc.,
361 Hanover Street,
Portsmouth, NH 03801-3912
Offices and Agents throughout the world.

Distributed in Canada by Reed Books Canada,
204 Richmond Street West, Suite 300,
Toronta, Ontario M5V 1V6
This edition is not for sale in Australia, New Zealand, or Europe.

CIP catalogue records for this book are available form
the British Library and the Library of Congress
ISBN 0-435-08681-2

Designed by Trevor Hood /ANACONDA GRAPHIC DESIGN
Printed in Australia by Robert Burton Printers, Sefton, NSW